Uncle Jimmy Jokes

By Jim Yezbick

TO SONIA
I HOPE
YOU ENJOY
THESE "STUPID"
JOKES.

Uncle
Jimmy

Afterword by Natalie Yezbick

James Yezbick, D.O.
ISBN-13: 978-1720599470
ISBN-10: 1720599475

DISCLOSURE

Nothing is original. My apologies to my wife, Susan, who is in despair over hearing my jokes over and over. No offense is meant to any <u>particular</u> minority or religion. The intent is to insult everyone. Also, please excuse any obscenities. This book is for adults.

I know all the jokes are stupid. That's what makes them funny.

Enjoy,

Uncle Jimmy

JAMES YEZBICK

AND SO IT BEGINS....

What did the Indian say when his dog jumped over the cliff? Dog gone.

Two psychiatrists were talking – an old psychiatrist and a young psychiatrist. The young psychiatrist was complaining the patients were all driving him nuts with their complaints. "These people just go on and on. They never stop complaining. I'm young, but I'm already sick and tired of hearing complaints all day long. Tell me: You're older and have been doing this a long time. How have you put up with it all these years?" The old psychiatrist replied, "What's that you say?"

A lady says to the psychiatrist, "I've got a problem. I think I'm a pair of drapes." The psychiatrist replies, "My God, you better pull yourself together."

A man goes to the psychiatrist and says, "I've got a big problem. I keep thinking I'm a dog." The psychiatrist replies, "Well, lay down on the couch over there and we'll discuss this problem." The man replies, "Oh no, I'm not allowed on the couch."

The man said to the dentist: "You have to pull this abscess tooth, but no anesthetic because I'm paying golf today and my tee-off

1

time is in 20 minutes. I don't care how much it hurts, but <u>no anesthetic</u>, understand?" The dentist says, "Okay, where's the abscess tooth?" The man then turns to his wife and says, "Honey, come here and show the dentist where your abscess tooth is."

I'm on a strict seafood diet. I see food, and I eat it.

"Johnny, can you spell 'before?'" said the third grade teacher.
Johnny says "B-E-E-F-U-R."
"No Tommy, can you spell 'before?'"
Tommy says, "B-U-F-U-R-E."
"No Tommy. Tyrone, can you spell 'before?'"
Tyrone: "Sure, B-E-F-O-R-E."
"That's exactly right, Tyrone. Now, can you use it in a sentence?"
"Sure, two and two be four."

Why did the Italians not have any shoes in World War II? Because they spent everything on defense and nothing on defeat.

Men are like fine wine. They all start out like grapes, and it's a woman's job to stomp on them and keep them in the dark until they mature into something you'd like to have dinner with.

I came home one night and found my wife in bed with the plumber. She said, "Please don't tell the mailman."

A 79-year-old man decided to have a facelift to look younger. Afterwards, he went to a new barber and asked him how old did he look. The barber replied, "Oh, about 47." The man said with a big smile: "I'm 79." Next day, the man went to McDonalds, waited in line, then asked the girl at the counter how old did he look. The

girl replied, "Oh, around 47." He said in a loud voice: "I'm 79."
Next day, he went to a bar and sat next to an old woman in her
90s and asked how old did he look. She said, "I'm old and can't
see too well. The only way I could tell is if I put my hands down
your pants and felt your balls." He says, "What? Are you crazy?
But okay." So they went to the back of the bar, and she checked
him out and said, "You're 79." He said, "That's exactly right. How
did you know? How did you do that?" She replied, "I was
standing in line right behind you at McDonalds yesterday."

A cat was crossing a railroad track, and a train came along and cut
off a piece of its tail. When the cat came home, he noticed a piece
of its tail was missing and went back to the railroad track to find
it. Another train came along and cut off its head. The moral of the
story is don't lose your head over a piece of tail.

A man calls a doctor frantically and says, "My wife is pregnant
and having contractions two minutes apart!" The doctor asks, "Is
this her first child?" "No, you idiot!" the man shouts. "This is her
husband."

Did you hear about the Arab who got sand in his date?

A girl called me the other day and said, "Come on over, there's
nobody home." I went over. Nobody was home.

What's the difference between a dog and a fox? About three beers.

When students took the entrance exam for medical school, they
were perplexed by this question: "Rearrange the letters P-N-E-S-I
to spell out the part of the human body that is most useful when

3

erect." Those who spelled spine became doctors. The rest are in Congress.

Q: Can you think of a car that starts with "P"?
A: Pontiac.
Q: No, Pontiacs start with gas.

What has 18 legs and catches flies? A baseball team.

What's the difference between an oral thermometer and an anal thermometer? The taste.

According to research, sex during pregnancy is always safe – unless your wife comes home.

"Do you talk to your wife after sex?"
"Yes, if there's a telephone handy."

How many fleas does it take to screw in a light bulb? Two. The real question is, how do they get inside the bulb?

An old man says to his wife, "Honey, I've got to get to the doctor right away on the expressway." He leaves, and his wife sees on TV that a man is going the wrong way on the expressway. So she calls her husband on the cell phone to warn him that a car is going the wrong way, and he replies, "Not just one car. There are hundreds going the wrong way!"

A policeman stops a man for speeding around a strong curve saying, "Not only were you speeding, but your door flew open and your wife fell out." The man answered, "Thank God. For a minute there I thought I was going deaf."

St. Peter says to a man at the pearly gates, "Welcome to heaven. You were good on earth and you can do anything here in heaven, but don't step on a duck or I will punish you for eternity. Ducks are sacred here." Well, the man stepped on a duck, and St. Peter said, "I warned you. Now you will be punished for eternity." St. Peter then handcuffed him to this 450 lb. female with bad breath, snot drooling from her nose, and warts all over. "You will be handcuffed to this lady for eternity," said St. Peter. Another man came up, and St. Peter gave him the same warning: "Don't step on a duck or you will be punished for eternity." Well, the man stepped on a duck and was punished just like the first man. A third man came to heaven and got the same warning but did not step on a duck. St. Peter handcuffed him to this beautiful blonde with a great figure and big breasts. He said to her, "How lucky I am. But how did you get handcuffed to me?" She replied, "I stepped on a duck."

The Norwegians, Finns, and Swedes decided to join armed forces for a better defense. They then put the navy on radar so they could scan da navy in.

If it weren't for marriage, men would go through life thinking they had no faults at all.

A lady says to her new friend, "I've been married four times. The first was a millionaire, the second a magician, the third a preacher, and the fourth an undertaker." Her friend said, "Oh, one for the money, two for the show, three to get ready, and four to go."

What food decreases sex drive by 70 percent? Wedding cake.

Papa Tomatoe says to baby tomatoe who is walking way behind: "Tomatoe, catch up."

A horse walks into the bar and the bartender says, "Why the long face?"

A skeleton walks into the bar and asks for a beer and a mop.

A termite walks into the bar and asks, "Where's the bar tender?"

What does a bottle of beer and a man have in common? They're both empty from the neck up.

The plumber says, "That will be $300." The customer answers, "That's over $300 an hour. I'm a brain surgeon, and I don't make over $300 an hour." The plumber answers, "Yes, I know, when I was a brain surgeon I didn't make over $300 an hour either."

An American lady who speaks a little Spanish goes to a bullfight with her fiancée, and afterwards they're in a restaurant where she orders "la especialidad del día." The waiter brings them both a large round meat, which he says are "cajones del toro" (bull testicles). They return a year later and again she orders "la especialidad del dia," and the waiter brings them two egg-size pieces of round meat. So she says, "Why so small this time?" The waiter answers, "Señora, zee bull doesn't always lose."

Wife: "Why are you so late from golf, dear?"
Husband: "Bob had a heart attack on the third hole and I had to

hit the ball then drag Bob, hit the ball then drag Bob, hit the ball then drag Bob."

The man asked the pharmacist if he had anything for the hiccups. The pharmacist reached over and hit the man in the gut. The man gasped in pain and said, "Why did you do that?" The pharmacist replied, "Well, you don't have the hiccups now, do you?" The man said, "No, but my wife does."

Did you hear about the optometrist who fell into his lens grinder? He made a spectacle out of himself.

What has two brown legs and two grey legs? An elephant with diarrhea.

Four Catholic ladies were having lunch when one lady said, "I'm so proud of my son. He's a priest and all the ladies have to call him Father." "That's nothing," said the second lady. "My son is a bishop and they all call him Your Grace." The third lady said, "My son is a cardinal, so they all call him Your Eminence." The fourth lady said, "Well, my son is beautiful and has a great body. He's a male stripper, and all the ladies just say 'Oh my God.'"

"Joe, how did you become a millionaire?"
"Well, when I was just a young boy I bought a pair of shoe strings for a nickel. I stepped outside the store and when I was about to put my shoestrings in, someone offered me a dime for them. I made a quick calculation and figured 100 percent profit in a few minutes was good. So I sold them but didn't spend the dime. Instead, I went back into the store and bought two pair of shoestrings for a nickel and sold them for a dime. I repeated this

over and over. Then a rich uncle died and left me millions."

"My shins are hurting me so much. I think I have shin splints."
"Oh, do you play football?"
"No, I play bridge."

The nurse says to the patient in the hospital, "Your urine looks a little cloudy today."
The next day she says the same thing: "Your urine looks a little cloudy today."
The patient was a little disturbed by her comments, so the next day he put apple juice in his urine collection bottle. When she said again, "Your urine looks a little cloudy today," he replied, "Oh, is that so? Well, let me filter it through one more time." He then picked up the urine collection bottle and drank all of it in front of her.

How do you keep flies out of the kitchen? Put a pile of manure in the living room.

How do you know when you've passed an elephant? You can't get the toilet seat down.

Why did the man not bring his girlfriend peas? He did not want to get her peas.

"That's life!"
"What's life?"
"A magazine!"
"How much does it cost?"
"Ten cents!"

"I only have a nickel."
"Well, that's life!"
And on and on amen.

The cow is of the bovine ilk. One end is moo. The other, milk.

"I see, I see," said the blind man, as he picked up his hammer and saw.

After all is said and done, more is said than done.

A good loser is a loser.

We spend our health to gain our wealth.
We toil sweat and slave.
Then we spend our wealth to regain our health,
Only to end in a grave.

There are no big problems – only small people.

Nothing succeeds like excess.

The old ladies in a nursing home decided to get into a little mischief and sneak outside and have a cigarette. So they went outside and were smoking when it started to rain, at which point one old lady pulled out a prophylactic, cut the end off, and slipped it over her cigarette. Well, the other lady looked and said, "What is that?" "Oh, that's called a prophylactic. I use it to keep my cigarette dry when it rains. I buy them at the drugstore." The next day the other old lady went to the drugstore and told the pharmacist she wanted to buy some of them there prophylactics.

The pharmacist said, "You do?" She replied, "Yes." "Well," the pharmacist said, "Okay, it's none of my business. How many would you like?" She replied, "Oh, about four dozen." The pharmacist said, "Four dozen! Wow! Well, okay. It's up to you. What size do you want?" She replied, "Oh, it doesn't really matter as long as it fits a camel."

One time I thought I was wrong, but I was wrong.

Age is a man's friend and a woman's enemy.

There are three ages we go through: Youth, middle age, and "Gee, you're looking great!"

There are two types of women: Good… and better.

Teacher: "Johnny, if you have four birds on a perch and a hunter shoots one, how many are left on the perch?"
Johnny: "None, the sound of the shots scares them all away."
Teacher: "Well, that's not the answer I expected, but I like the way you think."
Johnny: "All right teacher, I have one for you. If three ladies are sitting on a bench with ice cream cones, and one is biting her ice cream, the second one is licking hers, and the third one is sucking hers, which one is married?"
Teacher, aghast: "Well, all right. The one who is sucking hers."
Johnny: "No, the answer is the one with the wedding ring on her finger. But I like the way you think."

What has four legs, a tail, barks, chews on bones, makes little children happy, and is made out of cement? A dog – I just threw in the cement to make it hard.

There goes the happy moron.
Doesn't give a damn.
I wish I were a moron.
My God, perhaps I am.

To live with a woman is difficult.
To live without one is impossible.

Three nuns died and went to heaven. At the pearly gates, St. Peter greeted them and said, "We know you're nuns, but we do have laws up here. So I have just a little testing for you." To the first nun, St. Peter asked, "Sister, do you know the name of the first man on earth?" Sister answered, "Adam." And St. Peter said, "That's absolutely right. You can now enter the gates of heaven." To the second nun, he queried, "Sister, do you know the name of the first woman on earth?" To which Sister replied, "Eve." St. Peter said, "That's absolutely right. You can now enter the gates of heaven." St. Peter then asked the third nun, "Sister, can you tell me the first words that Eve said to Adam?" To which the third nun replied, "Oh, that's a hard one." And St. Peter said, "That's absolutely right. You can now enter the gates of heaven."

Man: "Do you know the first thing a woman says after having an orgasm?"
Friend: "No."
Man: "I didn't think you knew."

I know you believe you understand what you think I said, but I am not sure you realize that what you heard is not what I meant.

I don't lend money because it causes amnesia.

You can tell your girlfriend is happy to see you when you reach into her pants and it feels like you're feeding a horse.

A man goes to a bar, has a seat, then pulls his left pinky finger out of a closed fist, then his left thumb. He proceeds to dial a number into the palm of his hand. Then, he lifts the hand to his ear and starts talking into the hand like a phone. After he finishes his conversation, he puts his little finger and his thumb back into a closed fist position. The bartender, who noticed this entire event, came over to the man and said, "What was that?" "Oh," the man said. "I'm always losing my cell phone, so I had a chip put right inside the palm of my hand and now I can make all my calls right from my hand and never worry about losing my phone." The bartender replied, "I don't believe that," so the guy said, "Listen, I know it sounds unbelievable, but here, give me a phone number and you try it and see for yourself." So the bartender gives him a number which the man dials into his hand, lifts up the hand to the bartender's ear, and the bartender proceeds to talk into the man's hand like a phone. "That's unbelievable. I never would have believed you without trying it myself. Can you I buy you a drink?" The man replied, "Sure, I'll have a Jack Daniels and water." At this point, the bartender turns around, makes the man a Jack Daniels and water, and turns around to find the man is gone. So he asks a guy sitting next to him where the man went, and the guy next to him said he didn't know but he probably went to the bathroom or something. So the bartender thought maybe he had better check on him to see if he was ok. He walked over to the bathroom, opened the door, and saw the man standing there with his pants down around his ankles and a roll of toilet paper sticking out of his butt. The bartender said, "Hey, you ok? What happened?" The guy answered, "I'm fine." The bartender asks, "Then why are you standing there with your pants down around your ankles and a roll of toilet paper sticking out of your butt?" The guy answered, "I'm just waiting for a fax."

The problem is never the problem.
The problem is the <u>attitude</u> toward the problem.

Wherever you go, that's where you're at.

A bum sitting on a curbside says to a strollerby, "Hey buddy, can you spare five bucks for a cup of coffee?" The guy answers, "Five bucks for a cup of coffee? You know coffee is only a buck. Why are you asking for five dollars?" to which the bum says, "Look buddy, give me five dollars or don't give me five dollars, but don't tell <u>me</u> how to run my business."

A lady goes into a small store to buy a can of dog food, but the storeowner says, "You can't just buy a can of dog food like this. Some customers have been taking the dog food home and eating it. You have to show us the dog first." So later she returns with the dog, and the owner sells her a can of dog food. A few days later, the same lady returns to buy a can of cat food. The owner again says, "We can't just sell you a can of cat food because some customers are known to eat it. You must show us the cat first." After, the lady returns with the cat, and the owner sells her a can of cat food. The next day she brings in a small box with holes in it and shows the storeowner who asked, "What's that?" She replied, "If you will just put your fingers in the box, you will see." So he put his fingers in the box, brought them out with gooey stuff on them, and said, "That's smells like shit!" She replied, "That's right. I want to buy some toilet paper."

I had a real bad day today. It started on the way to work when I ran over a cat. I stopped to see if it was alive yet, but it was long gone. A lady came out of the house and told me it was her cat that I ran over. I felt bad and told her I would give her $20 for running over her cat. She started arguing with me that her cat cost a hundred dollars. Then her sister or someone came out with hair rollers in her hair and started shouting that a cat like that cost $200 today and I should pay $200. I said, 'Listen, I'm not giving $100 or $200. I'll give you the $20. I'm sorry I ran over your cat, but it was an accident.' Then while I was talking to this neighbor who told me they didn't pay for anything for the cat; it was given to them, one of the ladies went into the house and called the police. The police took her aside, started talking to her, and then asked me to come into the patrol car and tell my version of what happened. Well, I explained to the police how I accidentally ran over this cat, felt bad, and offered to pay the lady $20, but she wanted a hundred. Then her sister said she should get $200 for this cat, then this guy was there and told me aside that the cat was a gift and that the lady paid nothing for the cat. Well, the police listened to both sides of the story, then wrote me a ticket. The ticket said: for fighting in the middle of the street over the price of pussy.

A golfer is about to hit his two iron when he hears *rrrribbit, rrrribbit, three iron.* He looks around and sees a frog. He doesn't believe it but thinks why not, goes back to his golf bag, pulls out the three iron, and hits a perfect shot. Well, he thinks maybe this frog knows something, so he picks up the frog, puts him on the cart, and pulls out his seven iron for the next shot when the frog says *rrribbit, rrribbit, eight iron.* So he goes back and gets his eight iron, and this continues around the whole golf course. With the help of the frog, the golfer finds himself playing scratch golf for the first time in his life. He's quite overwhelmed, picks up the frog, and decides to take the frog home with him. In the car on the way home, he looks over at the frog fondly and the frog looks over at him. Then the frog goes *rrribbit, rrribbit, Las Vegas, rrribbit.* The guy thinks *Of course, Las Vegas!* He turns the car around immediately, heads all the way out to Las Vegas, and sits down at the roulette table at the Sands Hotel. The frog is next to him and says *rrribbit, rrribbit, 21, rrribbit, rrribbit.* The guy is now excited beyond belief, pulls out a hundred dollars, places it on 21, and it wins. He continues his bets all night, winning hundreds of thousands of dollars. The management offers to put him up for the night, and he accepts. He takes the frog up to the room with him, sits the frog on the bed, and the frog says *rrribbit, kiss me, rrribbit, kiss me.* The guy thinks *Of course, kiss the frog – a princess!* So he kisses the frog. "And that, your honor," said the man, "is how I got to be in this bedroom, incredible as the story sounds, with this 15-year-old girl."

A guy is playing scratch golf and is very happy about his game when he hits a tremendous shot on the 17th hole, but the ball lies right in front of this barn. He's scratching his head trying to figure how to get around the barn – over or around or what - when his wife who he is playing with says, "Honey, why don't I go down to the barn, open the doors, and I'm sure you can drive right through the barn." Well, the golfer is elated and wonders why he didn't think of this himself. So his wife goes down to the barn and opens the doors. He then hits a tremendous drive, but unfortunately the ball hits his wife in the head and she dies. A year later, the man is on the same golf course, on the same hole, and hits the ball in front of the same barn when his new wife says, "Honey, why don't I go down to the barn, open the doors, and I'm sure you can drive right through the barn." The man replies, "Oh no, don't do that, whatever you do. The last time I tried that it cost me a double bogey."

A guy is marooned on a small island for years. One day, he looks out and sees a small object on the horizon. He figures out it's a snorkel coming ever closer. Finally, a beautiful girl in a bikini comes out of the ocean onto the beach. He says to the girl, "Boy, am I glad to see you. I've been marooned on this island and haven't seen another human for years." She says, "You poor man. I can swim back to the mainland, and you'll be rescued, but before I go back, is there anything I can do for you?" The guy replies, "Well, to tell you the truth, it's been years on this island I haven't had a cigarette. You wouldn't happen to have a cigarette on you? But it's got to be a Camel. That's the only kind of cigarette I smoke." She replies, "No problem," reaches into her waterproof bag, pulls out a pack of Camels, and offers him one. Then she lights his cigarette and asks, "Is there anything else at all I can do for you?" to which he replies, "To tell you the truth, all these years on this small island and I haven't had a drink of whiskey. You wouldn't happen to have any whiskey in that bag of yours? But it's got to be Jack Daniels because that's the only kind I'll drink." She replies, "No problem," goes into her bag, pulls out a bottle of Jack Daniels and a glass and pours the man a drink. Now he's sitting there smoking his Camel and drinking his Jack Daniels, as content as could be. She looks the man in the eye and again asks, "Is there anything else – anything at all – I can do for you?" He replies, "No, that's it." She responds, "Are you sure you wouldn't like to play around?" He replies, "No, don't tell me you have a set of golf clubs in that bag, too!"

A reporter goes to China to interview a Mister King, whose first name is Foo. He knocks on the door of his residence and asks, "Are you Foo King?" The Chinaman answers, "No, I'm watching television."

A guy is sitting at the bar, looking real down. The bartender comes over and asks him, "Why are you looking so depressed?" He guy answers, "Oh, I'm down all right. I just came home today and found my wife in bed with my best friend. I was so angry that I got my gun and shot my wife." "Oh boy," said the bartender. "No wonder you're depressed. What did you do to your best friend?" "What did I do? I said to him, 'You're a very bad dog, and don't you ever do that again!'"

A guy goes to a psychiatrist and says, "I got a real problem. I can't remember anything."
Psychiatrist: "Okay, just lie down on this couch, and I want you to tell me all about this problem."
Patient: "Problem, what problem?"

Only a fool says he's positive.
Are you sure?
I'm positive.

An Irishman walks up to a black man at the bar and says, "Are you Irish?" The black man answers, "Oh no, it's bad enough being black."

After World War II, Hitler was found to actually be alive and hiding in Argentina in disguise. Some of his ardent followers went to him and begged him to come back to be their leader once again, but he adamantly refused. Again they approached him to return to Germany and become their leader again. Once more, he refused. Finally, after a third request to return, he replied, "Okay, I agree. I'll go back to become the new great leader of the world on one condition: This time, no more Mr. Nice Guy."

Abe meets Irving walking down the street and says, "Irving, how are you? I haven't seen you for years. What a lucky man you are that I should see you today because I've got such a deal you won't believe. It's a pet elephant, and I want you should have it, and it's only $100 for you, special." Irving says, "Abe, stop right there. I don't need an elephant." Abe: "Irving, listen. This is no ordinary elephant. This elephant is beautiful. It has a beautiful trunk. It can wash and iron your clothes with its trunk. This elephant can fix you drinks when you come home at night, fix you dinner, and even does an elephant dance, and for you the special price: only $100." Irving: "Abe, I don't need an elephant. I don't want an elephant. I live in a one-room apartment and have no use for an elephant, no matter what this elephant does." Abe: "Irving, I'll tell you what. I'll sell you this elephant for $50." Irving: "Now you're talking."

There are only two things to worry about in life: whether you're healthy or whether you're not healthy. If you're healthy, you have nothing to worry about. But if you're not healthy, you only have two things to worry about: whether you're going to get better or whether you're going to get worse. Well, if you get better, you have nothing to worry about. If you get worse, you have only two things to worry about: whether you're going to live or whether you're going to die. If you're going to live, you have nothing to worry about, but if you're going to die, you have only two things to worry about: whether you're going to heaven or whether you're going to hell. If you go to heaven, you have nothing to worry about. If you go to hell, you're going to be so busy shaking everybody's hand that you know down there that you won't have time to worry anyway. So why worry?

A guy goes to a dentist to have his tooth extracted. While extracting the tooth, the dentist slips and the tooth falls into the back of the guy's throat. The dentist moans, "Oh no. I'm afraid the tooth fell into the back of your throat, but don't worry, I'll just send you over to my friend, the otorhinolaryngologist, a throat specialist who can get that tooth out just like that. You won't have to pay anything extra, of course. He's just down the street." So the poor guy goes down the street to the otorhinolaryngologist, who does a direct laryngoscopy looking for the tooth and says, "This is bad news, but I can't quite reach that tooth with my instruments. It's already slipped down in your esophagus. I'm afraid you'll have to visit a gastroenterologist who will need to do a gastroesophagoscopy to get that tooth out, but don't worry, he's right nearby, and you won't have to pay anything extra, of course." So the poor guy goes to the gastroenterologist, who does a gastroscopy and esophagoscopy, then declares, "I'm afraid I've got some bad news. That tooth is now beyond where I can reach with my instrument. You'll need to visit a radiologist and get an x-ray. Of course, you won't have to pay and he's right nearby." When the radiologist took the x-rays, he exclaimed, "Take these x-rays to a surgeon immediately." The surgeon said, "It's already

down too far for me. You need a proctologist immediately."
Finally, the poor guy ends up in the office of the proctologist,
who's examining him and exclaims, "Oh my god, you got a big
problem. There's a tooth down here. You better get to a dentist
fast."

A lady goes to her doctor for her yearly examination. The doctor
enters the room and says, "You smell terrible. You're filthy. You
better go home and take a bath before I'll examine you." But
instead of going home, the lady goes to another doctor who says,
"Oh, you smell bad, and you're terribly filthy. Go home and take a
bath. Then come back, and I will examine you." The lady then
said, "That's exactly what the other doctor told me!" The doctor,
exasperated, exclaimed, "The other doctor! Why did you ever
come here then?" She replied, "I wanted a second opinion."

Two rednecks walking down a country road see this cow hung up
in this barbed wire fence with its rear up in the air. The one
redneck says, "Boy, I'm gonna get me some of that," and jumps
the poor cow. Afterwards, he says to the other redneck, "I'm done
now. You wanna get yourself some?" "Sure," said the other
redneck and went over to the fence, pulled his pants down, and
stuck his head in the barbed wire.

A guy goes to a golf course wanting to play golf, but the starter
informs him that club rules won't allow him to play alone. The
starter says he feels bad about the rules, but rules are rules. He
tells the guy he knows a girl who is also trying to get on, and he
could pair them up if he didn't mind playing with "a girl." The
guy said he didn't mind as he just wanted to play golf and didn't
care who he played with. So the starter fetches this beautiful lady,

who also happens to be a golfer. The guy is enthralled and on the 16th hole, he pulls the cart over and tells her: "Look. I'm playing scratch golf for the first time in my life. I'm just enjoying your company so much. If I par this next hole, how about I take you to dinner? Nothing sexual or anything like that. I just would enjoy treating you to dinner because I'm having such an enjoyable time playing golf with you." She replied: "Sure. But I would like to make a counter-suggestion. I too am playing the best golf of my life and enjoying your company as well. I suggest if I par this next hole, I treat you to a dinner at my place. I have a nice bottle of wine for us to enjoy. I'm a great cook. I'll change into something comfortable and whatever happens, happens." The man agrees, but on her third shot, she chips the ball into the sand bunker and he blurts out, "Oh, that's a gimme."

A man who works at a pickle factory confesses to his wife that he has this strange urge to put his penis in the pickle slicer at work. "Oh no, don't do it. I know you and those crazy urges. Just don't do it," his wife told him. Some weeks went by and he came home one day and announced, "I did it. I couldn't control it any longer, so I put my penis in the pickle slicer, and I got fired." "Oh no!" said his wife. "I told you not to do it. What happened to the pickle slicer?" "Oh," replied the husband. "They fired her, too."

A young man wants to be an actor. He goes to Broadway to find a part in a play but is unsuccessful. So he goes to off-Broadway then off-off-Broadway, but to no avail. He continues his search for days, weeks, and months, but all unsuccessfully. Finally, one day he lands a small part in a small theater. His only words to be spoken were: "Hark! Is that cannon I hear in the distant?" He's simply overjoyed with the news and goes home repeating his part over and over. At home he continues to practice his part before the mirror. "Hark! Is that cannon I hear in the distant? Hark! Is that cannon I hear in the distant?" Finally, the big night of the grand opening arrives. The theater is full. The play goes on. And now he is placed center stage in all his regalia and a cannon goes off. BOOM! He turns around and says, "What the hell was that?"

Jesus is going out to preach one day when his mother stops him and asks, "Where are you going?" "Oh, I'm going out to preach, mom." "Well, you can't go out like that. Go over and see Liebowitz the tailor and have him make you a nice jacket before you go preaching." So Jesus went to Liebowitz the tailor to have a new jacket made. When Liebowitz made him a jacket, Jesus was very pleased and said, "This is a really fine jacket. You know, I have 12 disciples and I want you to make jackets for all of them." To which Liebowitz replied, "Oh, you have 12 disciples. You must be a very important man. You know, we could make a business together. I can see it now. We could call it 'Jesus and Liebowitz.'" "No," Jesus said. "That name would never do." "Why?" said Liebowitz. "What name would you call it?" Jesus replied, "I would call it 'Lord and Tailor.'"

You can tell the nationalities of each guy at the whore house. The guy going in – he's a Russian. The guy inside – he's a Himalayan. The guy coming out – he's a Finnish. Now the guy standing on the curb across the street – he's a Polish. He's waiting for the red light to change.

What's brown and sits on a piano bench? Beethoven's last movement.

An old man told his wife that he was forgetting things and thought he should go to the doctor to find out if he had Alzheimer's or what. She told her husband she was having the same problem. She couldn't remember anything anymore, and she wanted to go with her husband to the doctor to find out if she had Alezheimer's disease, too. So the two of them went to the doctor and explained that they were very forgetful. After listening a long time to both of them, the doctor declared, "Listen, just write it down, write everything down." So the two went home and were sitting in the living room when the husband got up and announced he was going to the kitchen to make himself an ice cream sundae. He asked his wife if she would like one, too. She answered, "Yes, but be sure to write it down like the doctor said." He replied, "I'm only going to the kitchen. I can remember that. Do you want vanilla or chocolate ice cream?" "Chocolate, but be sure to write it down like the doctor said." "Oh, I can remember that. I'm only going to the kitchen. Do you want chocolate syrup or nuts on top?" "Nuts, but you better write it down. You know what the doctor said." He replied, "Don't worry. I'm only going here to the kitchen." So a half an hour later the husband comes out of the kitchen with bacon and eggs. She says to him, "I told you so. I told you to write it down like the doctor said." He said, "Why, what did I do wrong?" She replied, "You forgot the toast!"

A man falls in love with a girl named Wilma Ellis, and he is so enamored with her that he has her initials tattooed on his penis: W.E. He's very proud that he makes this commitment, and on his way over to show his new love his deed, he stops at a bar, visits the bathroom, and while urinating, looks over and sees the same initials, W.E., on this big black man's penis. He gets red in the face and says to the man, "Excuse me, but do you mind if I ask you exactly what W.E. stands for on your penis?" The black man replies, "Oh, that. Yes. Well, I'm from Jamaica, and when I get excited that comes out and says 'Why not come to Jamaica and have a really good time.'"

Spring: The time of year when the boys are feeling gallant and the girls are feeling buoyant.

I'm a very light eater. As soon as it gets light, I start eating.

I'm a very good golfer. I play in the low 70s. If it gets any hotter than that, I don't go out. A tribute to Uncle Lou.

What's the difference between a buffalo and a bison? You can wash your face in a buffalo.

A wife tells her husband that she doesn't want to play golf with him, but to meet her for dinner afterwards and be sure to play only nine holes and not be late for dinner. He promises to play only nine holes, goes off to the golf course alone, and is paired up by the starter with a beautiful blonde. They play excellent golf but after nine holes he apologizes that he has to leave. She invites him to her apartment to shower before he goes, and he accepts. When he comes out of the shower, she's on the couch in the buff waiting for him. He can't resist this temptation and succumbs to making love to her all afternoon. Then, he looks at his watch and remembers his promise to his wife. He races off to the restaurant to meet his wife and decides he can't think up an excuse and therefore decides to just tell the truth. His wife is obviously very angry and is pointing to her watch when he arrives at the restaurant. He explains to her how he was paired to play with this beautiful blonde by the starter and how after nine holes she invited him to her apartment to shower and then was lying on the couch in the buff waiting for him when he came out and how he just succumbed and made love to her, to which his wife replied, "You liar. You played 18 holes, didn't you?"

An old man tells his friend he paid $10,000 for his new hearing aid, but it was worth it because it works so well. "What kind is it?" asked his friend. "Half past four," he replied.

A man is put into an insane asylum and they take him to a recreation room where everyone is seated in hard chairs with no pictures on the wall. The room is void of everything, except the people sitting silently in chairs. After a while, someone stands up and says 67 and everybody laughs. A little later, someone stands and says 22 and everyone laughs. This continues on, so the man said to the person sitting next to him, "I'm new here. What's going on?" The person next to him replied, "Oh, we've all been in this institution so long that we got tired of telling the same jokes over and over, so what we did is we memorized them and assigned each joke a number. Now if someone wants to tell a joke, he can just stand up and say the number and everyone has instant recall and can then laugh at that joke." "Oh," said the newcomer. "Could I try?" "Sure, why not?" So the man stood up and said, "44." But no one laughed. Red in the face, the man sat down and asked his friend why nobody laughed. His friend said, "Well, some people can tell a joke and others can't."

A man is playing golf in Ireland and on the 13th hole he slices the ball into some woods. He goes out in search of his ball and sees a leprechaun in the brush. The leprechaun tells him it's his lucky day because he will make him the best golfer in Ireland, the richest man around, and have sex more than he could ever imagine. A year later, the same man is playing golf and on the same 13th hole, he slices the ball into the same woods and comes across the same leprechaun who asks him how he's doing. "Great," said the golfer. "I now play the greatest golf in Ireland. I always have an endless pocket full of hundred dollar bills, and I have sex as often as twice a month." "Twice a month! Is that all?" replies the leprechaun. "Well yes," replies the golfer. "But I figure that's not so bad for an Irish priest in a small town of 600."

Three things happen to you when you get old. The first thing is you start to forget things. I can't remember what the other two are.

Two guys are playing golf when one guy hits the ball into the rough where some buttercups are growing. He tries to hit his ball out of the rough but misses several times, becomes angry, and destroys some buttercups with his club. A fairy goddess appears and tells him, "You have recklessly destroyed my buttercups and therefore you will be punished. You will never have butter to enjoy. You will never taste it again. You will never see it or enjoy it again." At which point his partner is about to hit his shot, and he shouts out: "Be sure to stay clear of those pussy willows!"

A traveling salesman gets lost late in the evening far out in the country, so he goes to an old farmhouse, knocks on the door, and asks the farmer for directions back to town. The farmer says it's much too late to get all the way back to town now and invites the salesman to spend the night. The salesman is grateful and soon discovers that the farmer has a beautiful daughter. She fixes dinner that night and he falls in love with her. He asks her to marry him, and she replies yes because she wants to leave the old farmhouse anyway. He's enthralled and makes arrangements to return in one week to pick her up to get married. He leaves his suitcase and departs. The farmer is curious about his future son-in-law and opens the suitcase to find a suitcase full of ex-lax chocolates, which the traveling salesman sells. He doesn't know what ex-lax is but tastes one and loves the chocolate taste. Soon he finishes the whole box. One week goes by and the traveling salesman returns to pick up his soon-to-be bride. After he comes in the door, he feels an urge to go to the bathroom and his bride to be directs him to the outhouse out back. He goes to the outhouse and finds the farmer sitting inside but slouched over. He soon discovers he is dead, runs to his prospective bride inside the house and tells her that her father just died. She replies, "No, he died three days ago. We're just waiting for him to stop crapping so we can bury him."

The story goes that when the English first introduced tea to the Indians in this country, they promoted it as a health drink. The Indians were enamored with the concept of drinking tea for health and the story goes one zealous Indian drank gallons and gallons of tea that he died from it... He drowned in his own tea pee.

A good nun dies and goes to heaven where St. Peter greets her at the pearly gates and welcomes her in. He tells her now that she's in heaven she can have anything she wants. She requests to see Mary the Mother of Jesus, and St. Peter tells her he is very impressed with her holy request, but he tells her she need not be all so holy now that she was in heaven and that she could have anything now: food, sex, alcohol, everything was allowed in heaven. But she insisted that all she wanted was to see the face of Mary the Mother of Jesus, so Peter obliged and took her through beautiful celestial gardens until they came to a clearing with a long red carpet. The nun, elated, ran down the long red carpet to a throne and fell at the feet of the queen of heaven. Breathless and overjoyed, she kissed her feet and asked her, "Mary, please tell me how does it feel to be the mother of our Lord and Saviour, Jesus Christ?" To which Mary replied, "Vel, to tell you the truth, I wish he should grow up to be a doctor."

Do you know why Scotchmen wear kilts? Because it's amazing, but those sheep in Scotland can hear the sound of a man's zipper from miles away.

A blonde wants to get the dings out of her car, so she goes to an auto repair shop where a couple of Hispanics work. They decide to have a little fun with her and inform her they could fix the dings, but that would cost a lot of money and she could just do it herself by blowing hard on the muffler to get all of the dings out. So she thanked them for their advice, went home, and after the muffler cooled down, got down on her hand and knees and was blowing on the muffler when her blonde roommate came home and asked what in the world she was doing blowing on the muffler. "Oh," she replied. "These nice Spanish guys at the fixit shop told me I could save a lot of money by blowing on the muffler to get these little dents out of my car." "You dodo. Don't you know anything?" her roommate said. "For that to work, you've got to roll the windows up first."

Two good friends grew up together, went to grade school together, went to high school together, played on the same basketball and baseball teams together, and after finishing college, together both got married and went on with their lives. The years went by until one night late one friend called the other and said he had to see him right away as they hadn't seen each other in years. He was the only one he could talk to. So they met and the one friend told the other after swearing him to secrecy that he murdered his wife. The friend was astonished at the news and asked why he murdered his wife. His friend explained that it was only a short time after he got married and his wife began to nag and complain about everything. It gradually got worse until it totally obsessed the entire relationship. "Nag nag nag," he said. "She would nag me about everything. It drove me crazy. I got high blood pressure, ulcers, twitches, and insomnia. I couldn't sleep at night which got so bad I had to fantasize on ways to do her in. Mind you, it was only a fantasy, a game I played to help me sleep until one night I devised the perfect crime – the perfect way to kill my wife and never get caught – only now I'm feeling guilty and I need to confess this to someone, and that's why I called you, my best friend, to talk to. The way I killed her was I made love to her twenty times a night every night for six months and she died." "Remarkable – amazing," replied his friend. "What an ingenious idea! You're absolutely right. No one can put you in jail for that. You know, you won't believe this, but I'm having the same problem with my wife: nag, nag, nag. I'm glad you told me this because I'm going to do exactly what you did: make love to her twenty times a night for six months, and she'll be dead." The man finished his drink, said goodbye, and left. Well, six months went by and his friend was wondering what went on. So he decided to go over to his house to see for himself. When he knocked on the door, a beautiful woman answered the door, dressed in tennis clothes and appearing in very good shape. He gawked at her for just a moment, then asked if George was in. She said yes and took him to the back of the house where, lying on a divan, was this cachectic male appearing to be on his last breath. He could not believe this could possibly be his best friend and said, "George, is that you? What in the world happened? Are you okay?" George pulled his good friend's head down to whisper in his ear, "I'm fine, but I just feel sad for her. Look at her, how happy she looks, and she doesn't even know she's going to die tomorrow."

Father McCarthy was looking down one Sunday afternoon when Sister Anne Marie stopped by the rectory to look in on him. She asked why he looked so sad, and he explained he always looked forward to playing golf with Father O'Neil on Sunday afternoons, but Father O'Neil was sick and could not play. She said, "Well I play golf and I could play with you." So they went to the golf course and on the third hole, Father McCarthy missed a six foot putt and said, "Oh shit." Sister let out a gasp, and he said, "Oh I'm sorry, Sister Ann Marie. I forgot I was playing with you. I'm used to playing with Father O'Neil." Well, on the next hole he missed a four-footer and again said, "Oh shit." This time, Sister was in a tizzy saying, "Father, you promised." The Priest replied, "Sister, you are absolutely right. I swear, may God strike me dead with a bolt of lightning if I forget again." The next hole, he missed a two-footer and again said, "Oh shit." Suddenly a bolt of lightning came out of the sky and struck the nun dead. Father McCarthy looked up to the heavens just in time to hear a voice say, "Oh shit."

A guy is in bed with his sister-in-law and asks her for a kiss. "Oh no," she answers him. "We shouldn't even be doing this."

30

Why does a squirrel swim on his back? To keep his nuts dry.

What's a Grecian urn? About eight dollars an hour.

The three rings of marriage: engagement ring, wedding ring, suffering.

A guy goes up to a drunk at the bar and asks him to play golf. The drunk says, "What's golf?" The guy says, "Oh, it's a game, but let me take you out on the golf course and show you." On the golf course, the guy says, "Now, this is a golf course, and the purpose of this game is to hit that little white ball onto the green 405 yards ahead." "No problem," said the drunk, and he proceeded to hit the ball 405 yards onto the green. Well, the golfer was amazed as nobody but nobody ever drove a golf ball over 400 yards before. Still shaking his head with bewilderment as they came up to the ball, the golfer again explained to the drunk, "Now, the idea is to get that little white ball into the hole with the pin in it." "Well," said the drunk, "why in the world didn't you tell me that in the first place?"

Did you hear about the golfer who wore two pair of pants in case he got a hole in one?

What does a dog do that a man steps into? Pants.

What is the difference between a nun and a woman taking a bath? The nun has a soul full of hope.

"Doctor, I broke my arm in two places. What should I do?" The doctor replies, "Don't go back to those two places again."

Rectaloptitis: A condition where the muscle in your eye is replaced by the muscle in your rectum and you have a shitty outlook on life.

Customer: "Waiter, taste this soup."
Waiter: "Sir, I don't want to taste your soup."
Customer: "Just taste the soup."
Waiter: "Sir, I said I don't want to taste your soup."
Customer: "Waiter, just taste this soup!"
Waiter: "OK, where's the spoon?"
Customer: "Aha!"

"Honey, could you check the car. It won't start 'cause there's water in the carburetor." Husband: "What?" Wife: "I said the car won't start because there's water in the carburetor." Husband: "What are you talking about? You don't even know what a carburetor looks like. Where's the car?" Wife: "In the swimming pool."

A wise old owl sat in an oak. The more he sat, the less he spoke. The less he spoke, the more he heard. Now why can't we be like that wise old bird?

A man dies and goes to heaven. St. Peter greets him at the pearly gates and says: "Welcome to heaven. You have to pass a little test to get in, but I make it real easy. Just spell love." The man hesitates but then says: "Okay. L-O-V-E." St: Peter: "That's fine. That's all there is to it. Go on in." As the man passes through, St. Peter says, "Wait a minute. The big boss is calling me. Could you watch the gate for a bit? It's easy. Anyone that comes in here, just have them spell something easy like love then let them enter." The man says, "All right," then starts his watch. One after another as people approach the gate he has them spell "love," then allows them to pass, when suddenly his wife appears. "What in the world are you doing here?" he queries. She replies, "I was going to your funeral when I hit a truck on I-95." He says, "Oh, okay. Spell Czechoslovakia."

"Aunt Martha, you're ugly."
"Johnny, be nice and tell your Aunt Martha you're sorry."
"Okay Aunt Martha, I'm sorry you're ugly."

A lady stood up at the opera and shouted, "Is there a doctor in the house, is there a doctor in the house, is there a doctor in the house?" Finally, a well-dressed man approached her and said, "Yes, ma'am. I'm a doctor. How can I be of help?" to which the lady replied, "Have I got a daughter for you!"

A man looked over at his male friend, who was wearing a bra in the passenger seat of the car and said, "How long have you been wearing a bra?" His friend answered, "Ever since my wife found it in the glove compartment."

The different qualities of men and women:
     Women are honest, loyal, and forgiving. They are smart, knowing that knowledge is power. But they still know how to use their softer side to make a point. Women want to do the best for their family, their friends, and themselves. Their hearts break when a friend dies. They have sorrow at the loss of a family member, yet they are strong when they think there is no strength

left. A woman can make a romantic evening unforgettable. Women drive, fly, walk, run, or email you to show how much they care about you. Women do more than just give birth. They bring joy and hope. They give compassion and ideals. They give moral support to their family and friends. And all they want back is a hug and a smile. The heart of a woman is what makes the world spin.

Men are good at lifting heavy stuff and killing spiders.

That woman was so thin she swallowed a cherry pit and three men left town. A very old joke.

A man goes to confession: "Bless me Father for I have sinned. It's been six months since my last confession. Father, I confess I said the 'F' word." "What?" the priest says. "Where did you say the F word?" "I was out on the golf course and I hit the ball a country mile, but it got caught up in the high voltage wires." "Oh," said the priest. "That's when you said the F word." "No Father, that's not when I said the F word. A strong wind came along and blew the ball out of the wires. An eagle came along and caught the ball and dropped it deep in the woods." "Oh, that's when you said the F word." "No Father, that's not when I said the F word. Another eagle came along, picked the ball up and dropped the ball just two feet from the hole." The priest then said, "Oh no, don't tell me you missed the fuckin' putt!"

If I'm not in bed by 11:00, I go home.

Two old men talking: "My wife and I haven't made love in years. How about you?"
Second old man: "I don't know. I can't remember. What's your

wife's first name?"

An old man comes down the stairs with a suppository in his ear. His friend looks at him and asks: "What is that suppository doing in your ear?" At which point the old man pulls the suppository out of his ear, looks at it, and says, "Ah, NOW I know where I put my hearing aid!"

What does a toilet bowl, a laundry basket, and a woman's g-spot have in common? Answer: A man can never quite hit any of them.

Did you hear about the couple who met in a revolving door? They're still going around together.

Nine things you'll never hear a dad say:
1. Well how 'bout that? I'm lost! Looks like we'll have to stop and ask for directions.
2. You know pumpkin, now that you're 13, you'll be ready for unchaperoned car dates. Won't that be fun?
3. I noticed that all your friends have a certain "up yours" attitude. I like that.
4. Here's a credit card and the keys to my new car – go crazy.
5. What do you mean you want to do ballet? Isn't football good enough for you, sweetie?
6. Your mother and I are going away for the weekend… You might want to consider throwing a party.
7. Well, I don't know what's wrong with your car. Probably one of those doo-hickey-thingies – you know – that makes it run or something. Just have it towed to a mechanic and pay whatever he asks.
8. No son of mine is going to live under the roof without an earring – now quit your bellyaching and let's go to the mall.

9. Whaddya wanna go and get a job for? I make plenty of
    money for you to spend.

"Honey, if I were to die, would you give my jewelry to another
woman?"
"No, of course not sweetheart. I love you and wouldn't think of
that."
Later: "Honey, if I died would you give all my beautiful dresses to
another woman?"
"Don't be silly, I said I loved you and would never give your
dresses or any of your clothes to another woman."
"Honey, if I died would you give my golf clubs to another
woman?"
"As I said before, I wouldn't think of it. Besides, she's left-
handed."

What is the biggest drawback in the world? An elephant's
foreskin.

What is the difference between beer nuts and deer nuts? Beer nuts
cost over two dollars a pound and deer nuts are under a buck.

Doctor: "I've got some good news and some bad news for you.
The bad news is you have a unique illness and I'm afraid you only
have one or two days at the most to live. The good news is they
are going to name this new disease after you."

A man touring Egypt asked an Egyptian what he did for a living.
The Egyptian said, "I castrate camels." The visitor then said, "Oh
how interesting. How do you do that?" The Egyptian answered,
"It's easy. I get behind the camel, lift its tail, then smash his

testicles with a heavy brick in each hand." "Ouch, doesn't that hurt?" "Oh no, I'm always careful to keep my thumbs aside."

"Honey, I looked in the mirror today and I'm depressed because I'm getting old, fat, and ugly. Could you give me a little compliment to lift my spirits?" Husband: "Sure honey, at least you're honest about it."

"Father, I was very close to my dog, and he died last night. Could you say a funeral mass for my dog?" "I'm sorry, my son, but I can't do that. However, there is a nondenominational church just down the way, and I'm' sure they could accommodate you." "Thank you, Father. That's so kind of you. Tell me something – do you think a $5,000 donation would be adequate for the service?" The priest replies; "Jesus, Mary, Joseph – you didn't tell me the dog was Catholic!"

Why were Indians the first on the American continents? Because they all had reservations.

"Why do you have that banana in your ear?"
"To keep the elephants away."
"Does it work?"
"Well, you don't see any elephants, do you?"

Three Italian nuns die and go to heaven, and they meet St. Peter at the pearly gates. The first nun says: "I'ma not ready to be here yet. I'ma wanna go back." St. Peter says, "What? You want to go back? What do you want to go back as?" "I'ma wanna go back as Ingrid Bergman." St. Peter says okay, so she goes back as Ingrid Bergman. The second nun says "Waita minute, I'ma wanna go back, too. I'ma wanna go back as a Sister Teresa." So St. Peter sends her back as Sister Teresa, when the third nun says, "Hey, I'ma wanna go back too, as a Virginia Pea Pell Lee Nee." St. Pete says, "Virginia Pea Pell Lee Nee? I've never heard of her." The nun says, "No, she'sa famous. Look!" She then pulls out an old newspaper and shows St. Peter the headline: "Virginia Pipeline Laid By 300 Workers." – Rod

How did Statin Island get its name? When the Italians first came to America, they looked over and queried: Is Statin Island?

A penguin with car trouble pulled into the nearest auto repair and explained to the mechanic that the engine sounded funny and the car was not running right. When the mechanic said it would take an hour to check the car out, the penguin said he would go for a walk and return later. Well, it was a very hot day in summer and the penguin wanted to cool off, so he went to an ice cream store and ordered a large ice cream cone and continued his walk, but it was so hot out that the ice cream melted all over his face. When he returned to the auto shop, the repair man said, "You blew a seal," to which the penguin replied, "No, I didn't. I was eating ice cream."

To do is to be – Sarte
To be is to do – Aristotle
To be or not to be – Shakespeare
Do be do be do – Sinatra

A lady at the airport looks down and sees her daughter, who just got off the airplane arriving from Africa. Next to her daughter is a man dressed in a tiger skin. He has large earrings and a bone going through his nose. He's carrying a shrunken skull in his hand. The mother screams, "You never listen to me. I said marry a rich doctor!"

A man sees a sign in a restaurant window: "Lobster Tails $3.00." He can't believe it's only $3, so he goes in and asks the waitress if they really have lobster tails for $3. She reassures him they do and that they're regular size. He says: "Okay, I'll try one for $3." The waitress then brings over a chair, sits down and begins: "Once upon a time there was this big red lobster..."

A man sees his doctor regularly for headaches, but they keep getting worse in spite of a plethora of various medicines. He's referred to a neurologist, then to another neurologist, all to no avail. Finally he sees a headache specialist who, after examining him, says he is sorry, but he can't help him either. He then tells him he has heard of a small tribe in deepest Africa who have somehow had success with this rare and difficult to treat headache. The man, desperate beyond belief, gets on a plane immediately to deepest Africa where he finds this tribe. He explains his headache problem to the tribe chieftain who agrees to have the witch doctor treat him for these introducible headaches. Well, the witch doctor comes over and orders the man to take off all his clothes and put on a tiger garb. Then he has him drink snake blood in front of a fire while the tribe dances around him singing "Ooga-ugga ooga-ugga ooga-ugga." Finally, the witch doctor says he must submit to castration out of desperation. The man submits and is castrated with burning coals from the fire, and the next day his headache is gone. Overjoyed, he catches the next plane to New York, goes to a men's store still in his tiger garb, and requests a completely new wardrobe. The clerk looks at him and says, "You must wear a size 32 waist and 31 length in pants." The man, surprised, says, "That's exactly right." The clerk says, "And you must wear a 6 ¼ size hat." Again, the main is surprised and replies, "That's exactly right." Then the clerk says, "You must wear a size 16 shirt around the neck," to which the man replies, "Oh no, this time you're wrong. I always wear a size 14." To which the clerk replied, "My god, you must suffer from terrible headaches!"

A man seeks audience with the Pope. After waiting three days, he is finally granted an audience with his Holiness, the Pope. He bends one knee in genuflexion, kisses the Pope's ring, and begins: "Your Holiness, I am highly honored to make your acquaintance. I came to tell you I want to make a sizable donation of one million dollars to Holy Mother the Church. I'm not Catholic. I have money. All I ask in return is you turn the prayer to 'chicken.'" The Pope said, "Thank you my son, but I can't do that." The man then begged, "Please, your Holiness. I'm in the chicken business. If you would only change the prayer, you know, where you say 'Give us this day our daily bread' to 'Give us this day our daily chicken,' I will make it a ten-million dollar donation to Holy Mother the Church." The Pope replied, "Thank you. That's a lot of money and very generous of you, but I can't do that." The man then pleaded: "Your Holiness, I have chicken businesses around the world. Make that a $50 million donation. Just change the prayer to 'Give us this day our daily chicken.'" The Pope said: "This is a lot of money. I must talk to the college of cardinals first." So all the Cardinals gathered in the Sistine Chapel to hear the Pope, who said, "I have good news and bad news. The good news is I believe we are going to get a $50 million donation to Holy Mother the Church. The bad news is I'm afraid we are going to lose the

Wonder Bread account."

Upon finding a thermometer in his shirt pocket, the doctor exclaims, "Damn, some asshole has my pen."

A patient goes to a doctor with a cucumber in his nose, a banana in his ear, and a carrot in his rectum and asks, "Doctor, what's wrong with me?" The doc replies, "That's easy. You're not eating right."

What's the difference between unlawful and illegal? Unlawful is against the law. Illegal is a sick bird.

What's the difference between ignorance and apathy? I don't know and I don't care.

What island in the whole world has the lowest cholesterol levels in its populace? Statin Island.

A bowling team was in the finals of a bowling tournament, but one bowler didn't show up. So the other three bowlers on the team looked around the bowling alley but found no one except a decrepit old man bent over at the bar. The three bowlers, after some discussion, decided to ask him to fill in, although they knew if he knocked just a few pins down they would be lucky. With a quivering old man voice, the man agreed and with senile stance and gait, he finally got to the lane, picked up a ball, and threw a perfect strike. This continued throughout the game and the old gent rolled all perfect 300 games to win the tournament to the amazement of everyone. Afterwards, at the bar they asked the old boy what he attributed all this athleticism to at his age. He replied,

"Well, all my life I always believed in doing what I want. So I start every day by downing a quart of whiskey. I smoke, drink all day, and stay up all night." "Amazing," said one bowler on the team. "You've done this all your life and that's what you attribute all this athletic ability to. How old are you, anyway?" The old man answered, "Twenty-three."

What did the Jewish American Princess say after sex? "Peach. I think I'll paint the ceiling peach."

The teacher in 4th grade, who was fond of five dollar words, proclaimed, "Obsequiousness is typical of mendicancy." One little boy in the back of the classroom raised his hand and responded, "I'm afraid the superficiality of your phraseology is too copious for our diminutive comprehension."

A guy has an obsessive desire to be an actor. After several attempts, he finally gets an interview with the actors' guild, does a reading and is thrilled to hear he did a great job and is offered the chance to try out for a television role in a light comedy. When he told them his name was Penis Van Lesbian, he was told his name was unacceptable and he would need to change his name to something more appropriate. He refused at first, but unable to find a job anywhere, he relented and agreed to change his name. He became famous as the TV comedian Dick Van Dyke.

A Russian bought a new cow in a small town in Russia. He paid a lot of rubles for a bull to have her bred, but when the bull was placed behind the cow for breeding, the cow moved her backside away. This repeated itself. Each time the cow was placed in front of the bull, she moved aside. So the owner brought the wise man, a rabbi, to find out what the trouble was. The wise rabbi, upon watching the cow pull aside from the bill, said, "You bought that cow in Minsk." Surprised to hear this, the owner said, "How in the world did you know that?" The wise rabbi replied, "My wife is from Minsk."

A man is standing on the church steps with a long pole with a cross on the top and a tin can at the bottom. Not too far away stands another man with a long pole with the Star of David at the top and a tin can at the bottom. As the people come out of the church they look, then go over to the man with the cross and drop a dollar or two into the can. Finally, the preacher comes out, looks in both cans and notices the man with the cross has a lot of dollars, but the man with the Star of David has nothing, so he says to the man with the Star of David, "You know there's a synagogue just a few blocks away. You might do better there." To which the man with the Star of David looked over at the man with the cross and shouted, "Hey Moshe, he's trying to tell us how to make money!"

A lady playing golf gets hit by a golf ball. They take her to the emergency room, where the doctor asks where she got hit. Her fellow golfer replies, "Between the first and second holes," to which the doctor says, "Well, now there's hardly enough room for a Band-Aid there, is there?"

During the cold war, the Russians were competing with the Americans in the Olympics and were tied at 25 wins each with one event left: wrestling. The American coach took his young wrestler aside and said, "Look, this is the big event. You will be wrestling Igor the Terrible. Whatever you do, don't let him get you in the pretzel hold or you will never get out, and the match will end. The pretzel hold is where your right hand is behind your head, your left hand is behind your right hand, your right leg is behind your right hand and your left hand and your left leg is behind your right leg, your left hand, and your right hand. You won't be able to move at all. So whatever you do, don't get in the pretzel hold or the match is over and you lose." The young American wrestler replied, "Don't worry coach. Relax. I won't let him get me in the pretzel hold." Well the match began and bam! Like that, the American was in the pretzel hold. The coach threw up his arms in disgust and walked away knowing the match was lost, when he heard the crowd screaming. He turned around and saw Igor the Terrible pinned to the ground. 1-2-3. The match was over, the American won. To the cheers of the crowd, the coach walked away with his arm around the American victor and then he asked what happened. The American replied, "Well Coach, it happened so fast, I don't know. I found myself in the pretzel hold with my right hand behind my head, my left hand behind my right hand, my right leg behind my right hand and my left hand and my left leg behind my right leg, my right hand and my left hand. I couldn't move, I couldn't see, I couldn't breathe. But somehow I was able to open one eye just a bit and saw these hairy balls in front of my face. I knew then what I had to do. I reached out and bit down on those balls as hard as I could. It's amazing, you know, but when you bite yourself in the balls like that, you can get out of anything."

A man needs to use the restroom in a most modern, up-to-date five star hotel, but the men's room is occupied. He has to go so bad that he asks the concierge if he might use the ladies room while the concierge watches the door. The concierge agrees but warns him to not push the third button, whatever he does. When the man enters the stall he sees three fancy buttons. After he's done, curiosity takes hold and he pushes the first button. To his delight, a nice stream of perfumed water cleanses his bottom, so he pushes the second button and fluffy powder comes out. He's happy and against the prior warning pushes the third button, awakes in excruciating pain, all bandaged with the concierge looking down at him saying, "I warned you not to touch that third button. That was the automatic tampon remover."

A man asleep with his wife has a heart attack, dies, and goes to heaven, where St. Peter greets him at the pearly gates. The man pleads with St. Peter to send him back to earth because he's not yet ready to die and enter into heaven. St. Peter explains there is no one left to go back as, so the only way he can go back to earth is as a chicken. The man is desperate, so he agrees to return to earth as a chicken and immediately discovers himself in a chicken coop as a hen. He walks over to the rooster who explains he is now a hen in a chicken coop. He says to the rooster, "Why do I have this pain in my stomach?" The rooster explains he is trying to lay an egg and should push down hard, so he does and a beautiful egg appears, but he feels the pain again. So he pushes down real hard and another beautiful egg appears. He feels better and a bit proud when the rooster starts picking at his head, and the rooster's voice seems to change to the voice of his wife saying, "George, George, wake up. You're shitting all over the bed again."

As the man entered the doctor's waiting room, the front desk lady asked him why he was there. The man answered, "Shingles." So the front desk lady gave him some forms to fill out. After a typical long wait in a doctor's office, a nurse appeared and asked him why he was there. He replied, "Shingles." So she too him back, weighed him, and took his blood pressure and rectal temperature. After a while another nurse came into the room and asked why he was here. "Shingles," replied the man. So the nurse asked him to take off all his clothes, put on a gown and wait for the doctor. The man complied. When the doctor finally came into the room and asked why he was here, the man replied, "Shingles." "Where?" said the doctor. The man replied, "Out in the truck. Where do you want them?"

A man came up to another man sitting on a bench and looking so sad that he had to ask him what he was so sad about. The man on the bench explained he had this beautiful girlfriend who had a great figure, loved sex, and was always happy to see him. "That sounds great. So what's the problem? Why are you so sad?" The sad man replied, "My wife can't stand her."

German word for bra: Shtoppin von floppin.

German for virgin: Gutentite.

What has 18 teeth and a monster behind it? My fly.

"Dan, you have to stop masturbating all the time," said the doctor as he entered the exam room. "Why?" said Dan. "Because I have to examine you now," said the doctor.

Man to a woman at the bar: "Do you know what a 60-second sexual manic is?" "No," said the lady. The man replied, "Do you have a minute?"

Man: "Do you know the difference between a ham sandwich and sex in the afternoon?" Woman: "No." Man: "Would you like to go to lunch?"

A man goes into a bar with an ostrich, orders a drink for himself and a sandwich for the ostrich. The bartender says, "That will be $16.76." The man reaches in his pocket, pulls out exactly $16.76, and puts it down. The next day the man and ostrich go in the bar again. This time the man has three drinks and the ostrich has a bowl of chili. The bill comes to $32.37. The man reaches in his pocket, again pulls out the exact change. The bartender is amazed and asks him, "How come you can pull out the exact change every time to pay me?" The man says, "I stumbled on a rock at the beach, but it wasn't a rock but a magic lantern. When I opened it, a genie appeared and granted me three wishes. I wished for a solid gold Cadillac, and if you look outside, you can see my solid gold Cadillac. I then wished that I could reach in my pocket and pull out the exact amount of money I'd need for anything, and you saw me do that." "Wow," said the bartender. "But what's with the ostrich?" "Oh. My third wish was for a tall chick with long legs."

A man asked at the front desk of the doctor's office how long a wait to see the doctor and was told about three hours. He then left but repeated this query two or three times a week for several weeks, always leaving the office after asking. As this seemed strange to the doctor, he asked his assistant to follow the man to see where he went after asking how long the wait was. The assistant returned and told the doctor, "He went to your house."

A pharmaceutical representative increased his sales by over 700%

in one year and was asked to be the keynote speaker at the annual meeting. After his speech, someone asked how he increased his sales by over 700% in one year. He replied, "It was easy. I just changed one word when talking to doctors. You all know how doctors like to brag? When a doctor would say he plays golf in the low 70s, I would say 'Amazing.' When a doctor would brag his son graduated cum laude, I would say 'Amazing.' When a doctor would brag about how much money he made in the stock market, I would say 'Amazing.'" Someone in the audience then said, "So all your success was due to this one word, 'Amazing.' What did you used to say?" The successful representative replied, "I used to say bullshit." ☺

A renowned neurologist listened to his patient complain of unusual headaches that he had for years and nothing helped. After examining the patients, the neurologist related he had exactly the same type of headache and strange as it sounded, the only thing that helped was making love three times in a row to his wife. The patient said he would try that, thanked the doctor, and left. Six months later he returned and informed the doctor it worked and his headaches were gone. He also told the doctor he had a very nice home as well.

An older woman confided to her friend: "I think I'm going to have an affair." Her friend replied, "Well, I hope it's catered."

What do martinis and a women's breasts have in common? One's not enough and three's too many.

An old man and his wife visit the doctor. The old man tells the doctor, "We want to have a baby. We know we're old, but we still want to have a baby." The doctor condescendingly smiles and asks, "How old are you?" The old man says, "I'm 95, and my wife is 93." The doctor decides to humour the old man and instructs him to take a specimen bottle into the room with his wife and do whatever is necessary to get a specimen into the bottle. The old couple then go into the room and close the door. Shortly, the doctor hears screams, groans, moans, crying, and shouting in the room behind closed doors. This continues on for some time before the old couple come out all sweaty, hair messed up and looking entirely exhausted. The doctor queries, "Well, did you get a specimen?" "No," says the old gent. "We couldn't get the cap off the bottle."

"Where do you live?"
"Did you ever hear of a town called Armeens? Well, we live just beyond Armeens."

Cheer up, things could be worse. So I cheered up, and sure enough: things got worse.

The economy was bad for the small company with only two employees, Mary and Jack. So the employer couldn't decide whether to lay Mary or Jack off.

The golfer got caught in a downpour and ran for the car, but the car wouldn't start, so he put his golf balls in his pockets and ran to catch the bus. On the bus, a lady stared over at the bulges in his pockets and finally, out of curiosity, asked what was in his pants. The golfer replied, "Oh, I got golf balls." She then said, "I'm so sorry, that must hurt more than tennis elbow."

What is the best thing about deadly snakes? They've got poisonality.

What do you get if you cross a pig and a centipede? Bacon and legs.

What do you call cow with no legs? Ground beef.

What do you call a rabbit with fleas? Bugs bunny.

What do you call a bear with no teeth? A gummy bear.

A woman asks a doctor, "Can I get pregnant with rectal intercourse?" The doc replies, "Yes, you can. Where do you think lawyers come from?"

What do you call a dog with no legs? It doesn't matter what you call him because he won't come.

What do you call a hooker with no legs? A night crawler.

What do you call a herd of bulls masturbating in a field? Beef stroganoff.

A teenage boy had just passed his driving test and inquired of his father as to when they could discuss his use of the car. His father said he'd make a deal with his son: "You bring your grades up from a C to a B average, study your Bible a little, and get your hair cut. Then we'll talk about the car." The boy thought about that for a moment, decided he'd settle for the offer, and they agreed on it. After about six weeks, his father said, "Son, you've brought your grades up and I've observed that you have been studying your Bible, but I'm disappointed you haven't had your hair cut." The boy said, "You know, Dad, I've been thinking about that, and I've noticed in my studies of the Bible that Samson had long hair, John the Baptist had long hair, Moses had long hair, and there's even strong evidence that Jesus had long hair." His father replied, "Did you also notice they walked everywhere they went?"

It's too bad Arnold Schwarzenegger had this little misunderstanding because English isn't his native language: He told Maria that their housekeeper wanted a raise. Maria said, "Screw her." Any simple-minded, semi-literate Austrian could have made the same mistake.

Tired of constantly being broke and stuck in an unhappy marriage, a young husband decided to solve both problems by taking out a large insurance policy on his wife with himself as the beneficiary and then arranging to have her killed. A friend put him in touch with a nefarious figure who went by the name of Artie. He then explained that the going price for snuffing out a spouse was $5,000. The husband said he was willing to pay but that he wouldn't have the money until he could collect from his wife's insurance policy. Artie insisted on being paid at least something up front, so the man opened his wallet and showed him the single dollar bill inside. Artie sighed, rolled his eyes, and agreed to accept the dollar as a down payment. A few days later, Artie followed the man's wife to the local Walmart. There, he surprised her in the produce department and strangled her. The manager unknowingly stumbled into the murder scene, so Artie had no choice but to strangle him as well. Unbeknownst to Artie, security cameras recorded the whole thing, and a security guard called the police. Artie was caught and arrested, and he later revealed the whole plan at the police station. The next day in the newspaper, the headline read, "Artie chokes two for a buck at Walmart."

A blonde walks into a library. "PLEASE CAN I HAVE A CHEESEBURGER?!" she shouts at the top of her lungs. "Miss, this is a library," the librarian says. "Oh, sorry," she whispers. "Please can I have a cheeseburger?"

Jake was dying. His wife sat at his bedside. He looked up and said weakly, "I have something I must confess." "There's no need to," his wife replied. "No," he insisted. "I want to die in peace. I slept with your sister, your best friend, her best friend, and your mother!" "I know," she replied. "Now just rest and let the poison work."

A blonde lady motorist was about two hours from San Diego when she was flagged down by a man whose truck had broken down. The man walked up to the car and asked, "Are you going to San Diego?" "Sure," answered the blonde. "Do you need a lift?" The man replied, "Not for me. I'll be spending the next three hours fixing my truck. My problem is I've got two chimpanzees in the back that have to be taken to the San Diego Zoo. They're a bit stressed already, so I don't want to keep them on the road all day. Could you possibly take them to the zoo for me? I'll give you $200 for your trouble." "I'd be happy to," said the blonde. So the two chimpanzees were ushered into the back seat of the blonde's car and carefully strapped into their seat belts, and off they went. Five hours later, the truck driver was driving through the heart of San Diego when suddenly, he was horrified! There was the blonde walking down the street, holding hands with the two chimps, much to the amusement of a big crowd. With a screech of brakes he pulled off the road and ran over to the blonde. "What are you doing here?" he demanded. "I gave you $200 to take these chimpanzees to the zoo!" "Yes, I know you did," said the blonde. "But we had money left over, so now we're going to Sea World."

Two prostitutes were riding around town with a sign on top of their car which said: "Two prostitutes - $50." A policeman seeing the sign stopped and told them they'd either have to remove the sign or go to jail. Just at that time, another car passed with a sign saying, "Jesus saves." One of the girls asked the officer, "How come you don't stop them?" "Well, that's a little different," the officer replied. "Their sign pertains to religion." So the two ladies of the night frowned as they took their sign down and drove off. The following day found the same police officer in the area when he noticed the two ladies driving around with a large sign on their car again. Figuring he had an easy bust, he began to catch up with them when he noticed the new sign which now read: "Two fallen angels seeking Peter - $50."

A police officer pulls over an older woman on the side of the road.
Older woman: "Is there a problem, Officer?
Officer: "Ma'am, you were speeding."
"Oh, I see."
"Can I see your license, please?"
"I'd give it to you, but I lost it for drunk driving."
"Can I see your title and registration, please?"
"I can't do that."
"Why not?"
"I stole this car."

"Stole it?"

"Yes, I stole it and killed and hacked up the owner. His body parts are in plastic bags in the trunk if you want to see."

The officer slowly backs away from the woman and calls for back up. Within minutes, five police cars pull up. A senior officer approaches the car, half-drawing his gun.

Officer 2: "Ma'am, can you please step out of the vehicle?"

Older woman: "Is there a problem, sir?"

"Yes, one of my officers told me that you stole this car and murdered the owner."

"Murdered the owner?"

"Yes, could you please open the trunk of your car."

The old woman opens the trunk, which is empty.

"Is this your car, ma'am?"

"Yes, here's my title and registration."

"One of my officers claims you do not have a driving license."

The woman digs into her handbag and pulls out her license.

"Thank you, ma'am. One of my officers told me you didn't have a license, you stole this car, you murdered the owner, and his body parts are in a plastic bag in the trunk."

"I bet that lying bastard told you I was speeding, too!"

An Arab walks into a bar and is about to order a drink when he sees a guy close by wearing a Jewish cap, a prayer shawl, and traditional locks of hair. He shouts over to the bartender so loudly everyone can hear, "Drinks for everyone in the bar, but not for that Jew over there." Soon after the drinks have been handed out, the Jew gives him a big smile, waves, and then says, "Thank you!" in an equally loud voice. This infuriates the Arab. He once again loudly orders drinks for everyone except the Jew. As before, this does not seem to bother the Jewish guy. He continues to smile and again yells, "Thank you!" The Arab asks the bartender, "What the hell is the matter with that guy? I've ordered two rounds of drinks for everyone in the bar but him, and all that silly bugger does is smile and thank me. Is he nuts?" "Nope," replies the bartender. "He owns the place."

A man at a restaurant calls over the waiter and says, "What's this fly doing in my soup?" The waiter replies, "Well sir, it looks like the backstroke."

AFTERWORD

Well, you made it through. Read this book about a thousand more times, and then you'll know what it's like to be married to its author.

Behind these jokes are years of laughter, friendships, and love. Each one has turned a potentially frightening doctor's appointment into a pleasant one, a bad day into a better one, or a stranger into a friend.

My dad always said if you have but one good friend in life, consider yourself lucky. These jokes come from the myriad of friends, family, and visitors that have crossed my dad's path. From Brother Joe Yezbick to Joe McKane to Rodger Friedline to a man my dad chatted up in a restaurant somewhere, he's spent years writing down the punch lines on napkins and the one-liners on the back of businesses cards that found their way into this book. Thank you to everyone who has ever traded one of my dad's jokes for one of theirs, unless it's one of the really long ones. In that case, I wish you guys had never met.

Although my dad excels at his joke delivery, I know his true joy is less in executing the perfect pause before a punch line but in making someone else laugh and forget their worries for just a moment. Bringing a smile to someone's face is his favorite thing, and I am so grateful to him that he's passed that on to me. Hopefully I can tell a joke about priests and golf as well as he can one day.

Now that you've reached the end, I hope this isn't the last time you open up these pages. Just like my dad's jokes, this book is meant to be used over and over until at least one person has begged you to stop. But in true Jim Yezbick fashion, you probably won't, and your family and friends will be all the better for it.

Dad, thank you for years of giggles, for lots of material to tell at parties, and for having such meticulous handwriting. I can hear your voice in every one of these jokes. I count a lot of them as your legacy here on this earth because if I had to suffer through them, you better believe everyone else will have to, too. I'm honored to be your daughter.

- Natalie Yezbick

I should note that if I run for office, I disavow everything in here that offends you. Also, to use my dad's words: You shouldn't take life so seriously – none of us are getting out of here alive, anyway.

Made in the USA
Columbia, SC
24 March 2019